Live
&
Let Live

Live
&
Let Live

GERALDINE MULLANE

authorHOUSE®

AuthorHouse™
1663 Liberty Drive
Bloomington, IN 47403
www.authorhouse.com
Phone: 1-800-839-8640

Published by AuthorHouse   09/27/2012

ISBN: 978-1-4772-3064-0 (sc)
ISBN: 978-1-4772-3065-7 (e)

Any people depicted in stock imagery provided by Thinkstock are models, and such images are being used for illustrative purposes only.
Certain stock imagery © Thinkstock.

This book is printed on acid-free paper.

Because of the dynamic nature of the Internet, any web addresses or links contained in this book may have changed since publication and may no longer be valid. The views expressed in this work are solely those of the author and do not necessarily reflect the views of the publisher, and the publisher hereby disclaims any responsibility for them.

CONTENTS

SECTION 1
TEENS TO TWENTIES

The Old Man (Part 1)

Last night, the wind blew loud and fierce,
My hair did blow, my ears did pierce.
The trees were blowing, the sea was strong,
He stood there watching all night long.

The old man down by the sea,
Keeping his secrets from you and me.
He stands upon the pebbled shore,
But soon he will be there no more.

The summer comes, the people too,
He wants to hide from me and you.
When all is quiet, he will return,
For him I cry, my heart will yearn.

This mystery man you will not see,
Because he is an inner part of me.
I see him standing on the shore,
He will not last forever more.

When summer comes and I'm not free,
He will no longer be there, you see?
He will be gone, he will be free,
Because, he is an inner part of me.

I really want to let him go,
But how to do it, I don't know.
When I am walking on my own,
I want him standing there, yet unknown.

Oh please help me, can you not see?
That he is only imaginary.
Down by the shore, I need someone,
Who will make this mystery be gone?

Someone who is really there,
Someone who is always near.

The Old Man (Part 2)

I'm sorry I was not here yesterday,
My thoughts of you were so far away.
I walked along the pebbled shore,
And you old man, I saw no more.
Because with me, I had a friend,
My heart to keep, my soul to mend.
We walked together hand in hand,
Along the beach, down through the sand.
We talked of him, we talked of me,
And you old man, I did not see.
This is what I asked for before,
Until my friend is gone, I cannot see you anymore.

Temptation

The sun danced upon the sea,
Teasing you and teasing me.
For it is to school I call,
Although the sun shines for one and all.

The birds are singing,
Church bells are ringing,
The flowers are all in bloom,
But I must go to school soon.

When school is over, I'll come out to play,
And hope the sun will wait for me today.
I wish I was free to be out all the time,
Freedom from everyone, for me, would be fine.

Moods

I love this world, full of its dull and its happy moments
Boredom and surprises, its joys and its torments.
I thank the Lord that I am here,
In this beautiful place with my loved ones so near.
Tomorrow, I might hate it but that's the way it goes,
Today I'm happy, tomorrow full of woes.
We all have our moods, we're happy and we're sad,
Most days are good, but some days are bad.
When you feel you cannot smile, why not sit and cry
You'll feel happier again when you've cried yourself dry.
Never think you're not normal when you're feeling very sad,
I'll tell you it happens to everyone, does that make you feel glad.

Milan Abbey

The passageway down to the abbey,
The old church is just a ruin,
I will visit the churchyard maybe,
When the sun goes in and out comes the moon.
I walked around the rivers bank,
I collected some stones and flowers,
I threw a stone and down it sank,
And my happiness faded by the hours.
I listened to the birds call,
As I sat myself down on a stone,
I put my flowers on the old wall,
As I sat thinking on my own.

Looking Through

I look out of my window
The world is still,
A little bird perched
On my windowsill.
The little bird stares through the glass
My own dog barks, as he plays in the grass.
The sun is shining, and the air is clear
Today I am happy, today I have no fear.
Tomorrow is a day that will never come,
Outside the window is only beautiful for some
Look out through your window, and see what is there,
It could be foggy, or sunny and clear.

Hurt

I trust no one,
I have no fun,
I do not believe in anything they say,
I wish they would all go away.

I only say this because I am hurt,
I have been left with a broken heart.
I believed everything that I was told,
But I am getting careful as I grow old.

You said I was the only one for you,
But instead of one girl, you had two.
You told me to trust you, that we were friends
And when I asked about her, you tried to make amends.

Now, when someone asks to be friends with me,
I say yes, and wonder, what the catch might be.
So, if I say I trust you, believe me, it's not true,
I'll always think hard about falling in love with you.

Take Notice

Notice them, funny faces
In funny places.
Each one his own master, crying out for fun,
But this life of ours is one long rota
From day to day same thing after same thing
Over and over again
How dull!

Live & Let Live

Bright fresh mornings, I want to live more of it,
I tell myself this as here I sit.
Birds are singing, the wind is howling,
But, nevertheless, people are scowling.
What's wrong with them, are they not glad,
They don't seem to realise there's no reason to be sad.
What's wrong with blue, blue seas and lovely skies?
Forget the mysteries and forget the whys.
Live for today, love for tomorrow,
Only in your mind, is all your heartache and sorrow.
Forget past and future, aud learn from yesterday,
There may have been mistakes, but, come what may.
I may realise that my love is wrong,
But, what love do I know? Only the love I've heard in a song.
All the extra love inside, I want to share,
But no-one wants it so I leave it in the air.
I try to make you happy; I try to make you laugh,
But you just smile and bear it on my behalf.
I like to openly express my love and joy,
You think I'm not human, believe me, I'm certainly not a toy.
I wasn't programmed just to laugh and cry,
But I am going to forget that I ever learned to ask why.
If I'm so happy that I talk too much,
Well that's fine cos' I don't want to die with secrets and such.
If I'm sad then I'll let it show,
You don't have to be sad, just cos' you know.
If I like you I'll tell you straight,
Cos' if I die, then it's too late.
If I don't like you, I promise I'll try my best,
It's so easy, because you are simply a pest.
The world has its tall and its' short people

All so different like and elephant and a beetle.
We all have our good and our bad days, our ups and our downs,
We may find it hard to be a scientist but never a clown.
I live an experiment, the worlds just a game,
To experience living, that's why I came.
I may live life foolish, but that's my way,
If you think I'm wrong then why don't you say?
You are entitled to your opinion, and, I to mine,
And that's why we get on so well all the time.
Always be truthful, and say what's on your mind,
Forget the hypocrites and keep your thoughts underlined.
Don't hide true feelings, like joy and sorrow,
Understand what I'm saying and look forward to tomorrow.
If they want to change you, make sure you are not made,
Put down your foundations, and get your priorities laid.
Day by day, be happy and free,
So what comes next comes naturally.
Whatever happens, depends on fate,
So here I live and here I wait.
All my thoughts to the world I give,
There only one saying and that's
"Live and Let Live".

Hand Made

Blue blue seas and pastures green,
All across the land are seen.
The farmer ploughs across the land,
A land that was made by one great hand.
He sows the seeds deep in the field,
He hopes his future wealth is sealed.
He goes to the field, where his cows are grazing,
He has work to do, no time for gazing.
He has his wife and family too,
Sharing his love is what they do.
Their house is placed quietly on the land,
No city noise and rock and roll band.
The country life is far better for some,
When all they need hear is the dog bark and birds hum.

Dreams

Why do I see snowdrops in the spring?
Golden daffodils in the sky,
Pretty people who fly high,
A purple cow with a silver wing?

I'll tell you why, it's all a dream,
I close my eyes, I see the sight
Of everyone I know about to take flight,
But its' not as silly as it might seem.

Day by day, I live like a robot,
To be a princess is a chance I never got,
There are a lot of things I cannot do,
But when I close my eyes, my world is all new.

I fly high in the sky by day and by night
And I'm as pretty as can be,
Colours and sunshine everywhere I see,
I float like an angel I'm ever so light.

But when I wake up I'm sad once again,
I wish I could close my eyes once more,
But down to earth things are waiting at my door.
But I stop to dream every now and then.

But Names Will Never Hurt Me

I heard them whisper, it's plain to see,
That you're not the proper guy for me,
They laugh at me, they put me down,
When I sit thinking, they look and they frown.
They say I am unusual, offending and unwise,
They feast on the sight of you, and stare into your eyes.
They tell me to forget you, it's never going to last,
They tell me to put your memory far away into my past.
You said, "Your friends may leave you, but never will I,
I'll love you my darling, 'till the day that I die".
I never will give you up, as hard as they might try,
Because I think of the words you told me and know that it's no lie.
You tell me you love my face, as ugly as it might be,
So I ignore them because love is stronger than jealousy.

Food For Thought

We are fish of God,
Driven by temptation of the bait (money left around, cheating, etc).
We struggle for life,
If we avoid the temptation of suicide or fighting, We will live longer.
Like when the fish does not grab the bait, he Lives.
When people die, they have been hooked by God
And packed in a timber box, not like the fish we put in boxes.
Often when fish are caught by fishermen, other fish can do nothing it,
Even when they see them struggling
As when God decides to take a person,
No matter how hard they struggle for life,
We cannot stop it.

Boxes

They are fascinating,
In their many shapes and sizes.
Turn the key, what do you see?
Treasures hidden inside them.

I turned the key of the first,
This is what I saw,
Pencil, paper and an inkwell
And even some space to draw.

The second box was square,
But inside was the shape of a heart,
Velvet and lace, a locket fitted in place,
A jewellery box, how smart!

The third was mothers sewing box,
Needles and threads, thimbles and pins,
Covered in foam for a pin cushion,
Filled with wool, material and all sorts of things.

The fourth box was of silver,
With soaps and bottles of different scents,
It has no locks; it is mothers make up box,
But also holds some charms and pendants.

The fifth was a furry box,
Full of dolls, cars and bricks,
Placed inside the playing room,
Where baby plays his tricks.

The sixth was father's tool box,
A timber box of green,
With saw, hammer and nails,
And a green shelf in between,

So you see, these boxes are special,
With their little secret compartments,
Turn the key for they hold surprises,
They are full of joy and excitement.

If there was a box of smiles,
And I couldn't find the key,
I'd think of the joy that all the smiles would bring,
And I bet it would open for me.

A Poem to a Dying Woman

Lie dear woman in your bed,
Lay still and rest your weary head.
Right now your life is at a standstill,
You have no problems, try if you will.
Because when you are gone, your problems go with you,
You've no time left to do all the things you want to do.
You are heading for phase two of this human race,
You are about to beat us all to an unknown place.
You should be the happiest winner there can be,
Because your prize is hopefully, a better life you'll see.
When you get there, pray for us all,

Know we think of you when in our prayers we call.
You lived your life to the very full,
So at the end it must have been dull.
Because where you go now, we all dream about,
When we are happy it's a name that we shout,
Heavens above, God's sent his dove,
To take you to heaven to share his love.
The happiest woman you must be,
But we all cry when on your bed we see,
Your breathing has stopped; your body is white,
You left us all without saying, good luck and good night.

Apples of Love

Apples are like you and me,
The red of sweetness, the green of envy.
The heart is the difference as you will see,
All hearts can break so easily.

Our hearts will break but mend in time,
When the apple breaks, then that's the end of the line.
So if your heart ever breaks, remember your heart is not a core,
So wait around for what it takes, and soon your heart will mend,
I'm sure.

A Tribute

Steve McQueen, I see your face,
A portrait of you in earlier days.
I see your eyes so full of pride,
To be like you, I have tried.
The life you had, you lived to the full,
Yours so cheerful and mine so dull.
Your life was dangerous, wild and free,
A big adventure as far as you could see,
As an actor you made people laugh, you made them cry,
But the saddest act you ever did was to go and die.

Come Back

The air was fresh, the sky was blue,
I think of this as I thought of you.
To me you were everything, everything I had, everything I do,
But now I have lots more, I need nothing else, not even you.
The wind is blowing, the sea is rough, I think again, I think of you
I miss your loving, I miss your caring, and now I know,
I love you, I really do.
I'm sorry I offended you, I'm sorry I told you to go,
I wish you were here today, I'd tell you,
I love you, so that you'd know.

The Dragon

Late last night, a scene so rare
A dragon flying in the air.
A scene so rare you may ask why
To give an answer I will try.
The sky was blue, the clouds were black,
I saw the shape of a dragons back.
From his mouth burst a flame,
Don't be frightened he is tame.
Sun splattered colours of orange and red,
These flames I saw at the dragons head.
All kinds of creatures away up high,
Look for a farmyard in the sky.

The Wonder of it All

The misty blue of God's blue sea,
The emerald green of God's great pastures,
The golden moon behind bare trees,
The joy of loving God's great creatures.

The ocean waves express their anger,
All flowers blossoming with love,
The birds singing their sweet songs,
For this beauty ALL thank God above.

The City

The smoke, the smell, the dirty air,
The crammed up streets full of despair.
The endless noise, the constant grime,
Why is this place so dull all the time?
The lonely feeling amongst a crowd,
The traffic, the people, all so loud.
A polluted river, a black clouded sky,
With polluted bodies they all shall die.
Concrete buildings fill the air,
I'm facing facts, I'm seeing it clear.
Poverty and depression fill the streets,
Passing through beggars, drunks and cheats.
Look at how you live, is it very good?
Try and change it, don't just sit and brood.
Did I forget to mention, how thoughtless of me,
They destroyed nature, there isn't a tree.

Thoughts

O God I wish I did not think
Because I think too much,
O God I wish I did not think,
I've lost that trusting touch.
I think too much of this world O God,
Of plants and of living things,
I think too much of this life O God
Of how the dog barks and the bee stings.
I wonder how you made people so lovely,
Plants and animals too
I wonder how some are so lonely,
They have everything when they have you.

Why Live to Die?

The wind it blew
The sea was rough
I heard the gulls screeching
As they flew above
I came to the seashore
To think of a dead love
But my thoughts wondered
To God above
I wonder God why you made us so,
To love and be loved
To think and be thought of
To comfort and be comforted
To laugh and to cry
To live and to die?

Conor

Little baby boy, innocent child so full of grace,
All the problems in this world are miles away
from your smiling face.
When I'm down, I just look at you
Because your laughter is sincere and true.
You don't need words; your actions say you are glad
You are praised when you are good and pitied when you are bad.
All your decisions people make for you
There's no need to think, they do that too.
Your face and your hair, so soft and so pure,
A face so like your father's and brothers before.
Keep that smile and play your games
Know no places and know no names.
Things of the world you soon will learn
When that time comes, your happy childhood you will yearn.
O mother dear, do not ruin this child,
Let him run free, let him run wild.
Keep your problems until his childhood is past,
Keep him young and don't let him grow up too fast.
I'm envious of him; it's easy to be,
When I look at him, his smile and soft face is all that I see.
He is so trusting he holds out his hands,
He knows of no enemies, only of friends.
When he walks and talks and moves his head,
It's so natural, we do it until the day we are dead.
But this child might yet discover something new,
Something that his children might naturally do.
He could be a teacher, a scientist or the pope,
His future is uncertain, and yet, so full of hope.

First Impressions

First impressions are what it takes
First impressions are what you make.
I looked at a person and liked what I saw
I saw some goodness and certainly no flaw.
She had a heart of gold and a head of steel,
A heart that was broken and wouldn't heal.
She loved a person, who was beyond her reach,
Her suffering was in her actions and also in her speech.
She formed a smile but her eyes were sad,
She wondered would this world always be so bad.
I wanted her to be friends with me,
She tried her best as far as I could see.
I was so sad I could take no more,
And my sadness didn't help hers I'm sure.
But I know someone who can help her in her long lonely days,
Someone who understands her in so many ways.
He loves her as much as the sun in the sky
Why they can't be together, he'll never know why.
They have a love that is good, so happy and strong,
A love that is right and yet always so wrong.
If I could tell you her story as it goes,
Then she would have friends in everyone who knows.
Friends, who would make her laugh whenever she'd cry,
Friends to persuade her she has to get by.
She has to keep smiling in a world that's not so good,
She has to see her problem as other people would.
It was a love that was delivered from inside God's gate,
A love that sadly came too late.
I wish I could make her laugh as much as she can,
But her laughter got lost in her love of a man.
He has never died and is still around,

So be happy to know that he can be found.
There is nothing worse than a love in the grave,
But this love is living, so you must be brave.
Know in your mind that he will never leave you,
Know that he is with you in everything you do.
Keep a happy face; keep your head in the air,
I know it is sad, it is all so unfair.
If I could only practice what I preach,
Then the answers to the whole world I would teach.
It's easy to say, but very hard to do,
I hope that you understand that too.
I know that I'm not a friend; I don't know you very well,
But let me share your problems, and I'll chase them all to hell.
There's a world out there waiting, just waiting for you,
It's waiting until you decide what to do.
It's full of good people and bad ones a few,
If you let them help you, I know you'll pull through.
So cry for an hour then laugh until the end,
I know you may not like me, but, I am a friend.
A friend who will follow the course of your health,
Someone who understands exactly how you felt.
My first impressions are ones that stay,
And you are a lovely person in every way.

The Higher you go the Harder you Fall

You understand all that I'm saying,
You know the price my heart is paying.
You go around easing pain,
You are unselfish and also unvain.
You say all the right things that have to be said,
You keep people's problems deep inside your head.
You go around helping people like me,
You listen to their problems, no matter what they might be.
You have problems of your very own,
But you keep them bottled up until you are alone.
Why don't you share your problems with one and all,
Then we will understand you whenever you call.
There is no need to be a friend to everyone you greet,
They throw at you every problem that they meet.
They take advantage of your good nature and heart,
With their lives full of worries they'll tear you apart.
You sit like a saint and take it all in,
You listen with patience from the time they begin.
You give them the comfort they so greatly desire,
You ease their sore minds and put out the fire.
They have given all their worries to you,
Their heart is so light it feels like it's new.
Sometimes you know you told them a lie,
But deep in your heart you know they'll get by.
Because you understand that big bend in the road,
And you know that when you get around it you'll unburden the load.
But they can't get past that great big old bend,
So you are their driver right until the end.
Remember that you have a life of your very own,
So sort out your problems and keep that life going.
You have eyes that penetrate deep into a soul,

When you see people falling you fill in the hole.
You help them to keep their feet firmly on the ground,
They know that when they are worried that you are around.
Everyone needs someone to help them along,
They need to be told where they go wrong.
But do you know anyone that is so much like you,
That when you are troubled they will know what to do.
Someone who will sit and listen to all that you say,
Someone you care for, who'll brighten your day.
So we'll give you a break to do your own thing,
But we'll always remember the happiness you bring.
So let's reverse the roles and you sit and talk,
But remember you have friends wherever you walk.
People who know the true side of you,
Always some old friends and certainly some new.
You have a charm that's unique and rare,
A charm that can be abused, so always beware.
Beware of the people, who take what they can,
Who'll take advantage of a very fine man.
Remember that the higher you go, the harder you fall,
So friend, don't go running whenever they call.

Please Keep in Touch,
We Miss You So Much

Some time ago I promised you I'd write you a simple line,
A line that would always be a memory of yours and a memory of mine.
But the time has gone and now it's too late,
But you can take this poem with you, if your soul will wait.
Please wait in silence while I write about you,
About all the things you learnt and all the things you knew.
You knew how to be kind, generous and great,
You knew how to be honest, so forward and straight.
You told me a story and I listened with joy,
And at that very moment my sadness you could destroy.
You have a family that are so much the same,
They carry your greatness, not only your name.
You'll always be remembered for all that you've done,
I'll always remember you, even though you are gone.
The sadness in me goes deep down inside,
But you are happy because Gods arms are open wide.
I have no doubt that it is to God you'll go,
Because you were an Angel when you were below.
When you meet God, ask him to pray for us all,
Because we will be crying when we see your coffin fall.
I couldn't write a happy poem, it's very hard to do,
The only happiness I can imagine is if you were here too.
One day we'll all meet in that great land above,
And I hope that then you will be as generous with your love.
A love that was good and always so strong,
A love that told people that they belong.
They belong in this world and never too much,
You gave them the confidence because you had the touch.
The touch of a healer and an Angel combined,

A touch that helped people have gladness on their mind.
Every day you'd go for a walk,
And every day you'd stop for a talk.
You would talk of the weather, if it was hot or if it was cold,
You would talk about life and all the things it could hold.
I promised myself I would meet you some more,
But I never kept that promise and now my conscious is sore.
It's sore from the fact that I wasn't too nice,
But now in my regret I am paying the price.
I lie in bed at night and dream about you,
And wonder what exactly it is that you do.
This world I am sure was made for you old man,
Because you were always happier than the young people plan.
There is one thing that I have to tell you before I go,
It's one important thing that you should know.
Your family are sad and they miss you so much,
But I hope that through this poem, you will always stay in touch.

For Ethel on her 12th Birthday

Enjoy your youth, run wild and free,
Look all around and what do you see,
People are down, their faces are long,
Fight all their opinions while you are strong.
They want to make you as unhappy as can be,
They try it on everyone; they've tried it on me.
They think they are right, but what do they know,
If you want to be different, then let it be so.
I don't mean be selfish and think only of you,
There are some sad people, think of them too.
They have made mistakes, they cannot go back,
Pride in themselves is all that they lack.
If they are so ignorant they glare at you,
Smile at them gracefully, that's what I do.
It's easy to be envious of someone who is free,
Pity their envy and just let it be.
You have your good looks and graciousness too,
You have the choice to do something new.
If they frighten you by telling you you're wrong,
Don't let them capture you, they'll drag you along.
They'll drag you down to the depths of despair,
I really love you but I can't always be there.
I have to get away from this ugly filled place,
I look at my life and cry in disgrace.
I've let all my moods overrule my days,
And now I am different in so many ways.
I always keep secrets engraved on my mind,
But when I am angry, I have to unwind.
I unwind in a poem that is so full of bad news,
I write it to anyone or anything that I choose.
My freedom is got from all that I write,

Yours could be got from dancing all night.
You have to choose your very own things,
You have to know life and all that it brings.
You have to decide what kind of person you are,
Then you must make that person way better by far.
If you see someone you think is brighter than you,
Please don't try to copy them and do as they do.
Remember this warning right from the start,
There are no two people you cannot tell apart.
God made us all to be someone new,
He didn't make me just to be like you.
He wants separate people to be happy and bright,
He doesn't want shadows, some dark and some light.
When you are young, you are happy and you are sad,
Your life is so good and then suddenly so bad.
But when you get older, you are not so confused,
You know life is for living and has to be used.
You remember all the problems you had so long ago,
And now all the answers you suddenly do know.
You'll find all the answers as the years move along,
You'll survive in this world if only you are strong.
So be your own person and do what you can,
You'll be a happier person in this world made for man.
Keep this poem engraved on your mind,
And one day some answers in it you'll find.

Birds of a Feather

It's bright outside but dull in here,
My mind is foggy but the air is clear.
I'm not focusing on the world outside,
But I'm thinking desperately of the turmoil inside.
I have problems, some old and some new,
I know what is needed; I know what I should do.
I should start again, a new life, I'm sure,
But if this one went wrong, I could take no more.
The solutions are simple, but the actions are not,
You take all I give but what have I got.
My mind is so weak and so full of despair,
You think you love me, but its' really not fair.
If you loved me, you'd always be near,
But being alone without you, I have to bare.
My nature is to give, to love and adore,
Yours is for beauty and you always want more.
I want to be someone you are proud to have around,
But I am an ugly duckling who got lost and hasn't been found.
Why don't you take me for what I am?
Then I'd be a happier person and you a happier man.
We'd spend our lives sharing and loving together,
We'd never need words; we'd be like birds of a feather.
You'd do for me, and I'd do for you,
Our good times would be many and our bad ones so few.
We were made for each, you cannot deny,
We could blend together if only you'd try.
You think you are so young, you should be happy and free,
But there are two youths involved, and one of them is me.
If there were three lives, would things be the same,
I would be baring the child that bares your name.
Would you swear to love me until death do us part?

Would this child help you to know what you should have known
from the start?
If this is the case, you never will know,
Because me and your child will pack up and go.
I'll have part of you and that's all I need,
Call it true love but don't call it greed.
You can have permission to see your child in years to come,
By then I hope you are married and raising a son.
A son you can tell that love is for two,
Loving her, as much as she loves you.

SECTION 2
THIRTY SOMETHING

Dear John

The doctor said that all was fine and I am well,
That I wouldn't die and go to hell.
He said that I had a long time yet to live,
So all my spare happiness to you I'll give.
Because you were the one who told me to be strong,
You were the one who helped me along.
You were the one, who gave me new life,
And because of me you neglected your poor wife.
Tell her to forgive you, that I was to blame,
You had a good excuse although it might sound lame.
I told you I was dying and that I felt down,
And for your great help I'll give you a crown.
A crown to say that you are the King of all hope,
A King who says that everyone should be happy
and no-one should mope.
You know that this letter could drag on for days,
I have to say thank you in so many ways.
I could write a book on all you did for me,
But when you'd finish reading it, an old man you'd be.
I won't give any details of my sad, sad old life,
My life full of worries and struggle and strife.
You should know it now as well as your own,
So thanks all the same I have to be going.
I am going to finish this right here and right now,
How the pen left the paper, I'll never know how.

Pat

Pat you old fool you broke my heart,
The day that you died and tore my sister apart.
You came into our lives and filled them with care,
Because all the love you had you'd so freely share.

I really got to know your family after you were gone,
Then I realised where your love had come from.
Your family are so loving, close and kind,
A family that loves each other so much is hard to find.

Every time we met we had a great chat,
And you will always be my Farmer Pat.
You were the type that I could talk to all night long,
The last chat we had continued till daylight had come.

That night I knew I was pregnant and told you so,
I was feeling frightened, lonely and terribly low.
You made me realise I wasn't alone,
And I was always welcome into your home.

I thank you for the confidence you gave to me,
And how you and Ethel helped me through my pregnancy.
If you could see Amy now you'd love her to pieces,
Because she is so sweet and happy and she is one of your nieces.

Her godfather you should have been,
But now I am asking you to be her Guardian Angel if you are keen.
Ethel is brilliant and loves her like her own,
But I wish she didn't have to do this alone.

There is no point in dwelling in the past,
Your being in our lives was beautiful to the last.
A year has nearly gone by since you went,
And in our hearts your place is just one big dent.

We miss you, we love you, and we wish you were here,
But we have to live on until we meet you there.
Keep the bar stool warm for me,
I'll bring Ethel and you can call the drinks for three.

I'm glad of the memories you gave to my life,
And I thank you for having my sister as your wife.
We'll look after Ethel as much as we can,
But it's hard to reach her since she lost her one and only man.

Take care, good luck, happy next life,
Look out for your family and especially your wife.
Say Hi to everyone we've lost over the years,
And every time we think of you we'll shed a few tears.

"Teletubbies please say Bye, Bye"

The Teletubbies were being bold.
Listen mum! To what they are being told
It wasn't me that was doing wrong,
You just don't know what was going on.
I went to say bye, bye, I even said day, day,
But they just wouldn't go away.
I thought it was time for them to go to bed,
And it was definitely time for me to be fed.
You always turn them on to say bye, bye,
Why they didn't I don't know why.
My old pal La La hopped around the green,
As I waited for the ads to come on the screen.
My tummy said "Kell let's go",
What to do I didn't know.
I waved day, day and blew a kiss,
But I think it must have been a miss.
They didn't answer, they didn't hear,
My tummy started to fill with fear.
What if they never went and stayed all day,
Then I'd miss my dinner and anything else that might come my way.
So I went a bit closer and told them to go,
But would they leave, by God, Oh No!
So I smacked their hands and heard a bang,
And that is when the doorbell rang.
Paul had come to play with me,
But you wouldn't believe what you could see,
The tele was hissing loud and sparking mad,
But the Teletubbies were gone and I was glad.
I put my arms up to demand my food
But you looked as if you had a mouthful of something that
couldn't be chewed.

Your face was red; your eyes were alight,
By golly, but you were an ugly sight.
You jumped around, and Aunt Mary too,
You looked like you needed to go to the loo.
There was no dinner, there was no smell,
And I was thinking that I wasn't doing too well.
I bawled and bawled and made you look,
And I wanted to say why don't you cook.
Mum, I put the Teletubbies to bed,
I'm such a good girl, I deserve to be fed.
You picked up the phone and called my dad,
When he arrived, boy was I so glad.
This is the man, who'll make me my dinner,
I think I might be on to a winner.
He stayed in the room and looked at the flame,
And from him a funny sound came.
I wish I could talk, I do my best,
But when I'm older I'll tell you the rest.

Three of a Kind!!!

Leon, Beck and Denis went out one day,
Over the hills and far away.
I'm only joking; they went to the park,
But then they came back because it was too dark.
They sat in all day planning what to do,
Where they'd go and who'll go with who?
Each wanted to do a different thing
I bet this has a familiar ring.
By the time they had made up their minds,
Street lights were on and people were pulling their blinds.
They went for a walk and ended up in the park,
But as I said already it was too dark.
So they spent the night planning the next day,
But I'd give you a guess where they went to play.
They stayed at home planning what to do,
But with Leon, Beck and Denis that's nothing new.
As the saying goes "three of a kind",
But that's not exactly what I had in mind.
They refuse to agree and can waste a whole day,
Deciding how to have fun and where to play.
One wants to go left, the other go right
and the other just doesn't care,
But all children are like that as far as I am aware.
So don't worry lads you'll get it right some day,
Probably when you're all too old to go out and play.
So go out now and have some fun,
It's better that staying at home with dad and mum.
Take it in turns to say where to go,
And let the rest just "go with the flow".

My Circle of Friends

My circle of friends are precious to me,
Each one unique and needed so differently.
I adore you all different days of the week,
The mad ones, the strong ones and the ever so weak.

You all suit a side of me depending on my day,
And I need each one of you in a different way.
I treasure you, adore you and care for you so much,
Because to me you are such a wonderful bunch.

Each one of you doesn't know who else is there,
But, because you are all there for me is all that I care.
We touch each other's lives in different ways
We may not see each other for months or even for days.

But even when we neglect to keep in touch,
You are always in my thoughts ever so much.
A New Year is on the way that will bring new hope,
And as we have each other we will always manage to cope.

As you are a special friend and are always there for me,
I give you this little gift which is filled with my identity.
I hope you enjoy it and it brings lots of pleasure,
Because to have a friend like you is a God given treasure.

The Walker

I wondered through the woodlands, walking on my own,
People did not realise that I wanted to be alone.
They stopped beside me to pass the time of day,
But I only wanted to say goodbye and then be on my way.
It is a habit of nature to feel for someone
who looks as if they have no-one to care,
They walk without a partner and we think
that with us they'd like to share.
We want to share their feelings
and let them know that friends are there,
Sometimes this isn't necessary, as there are other reasons
that we are not aware.
I sometimes like to leave my home and head for a long walk,
The last thing I really want is to have someone
come along for a talk.
I spend my days listening to the chatter of my family,
But there are certain days when I'd like no chatter
and just listen to ME.
I need to keep in touch with the person that's inside,
With the busy life I lead that person stays ahide.
So often when I have time to spare I like to stretch my feet,
I tune into my thoughts and let my feelings have a treat.
I clear the cobwebs from my otherwise clogged up mind,
And when I return home, I feel more inclined to be kind.
I have given me the time that I need to let my body recharge,
And helps me to handle my children, my house, and my life at large.
So the next time you see a lone walker,
don't rush to keep them company,
A smile will let them know you care and the rest can only be.
A decision that they will make depending on their mood,
They may want to stop and talk or continue through the wood.

To My Unknown and Unnamed

Why were you taken away from me?
How come you I will never see?
Why was God so cruel to take you away?
When I was so looking forward to you coming to stay.

I want to know if you were a girl or a boy,
To hold you in my arms, now I will never know the joy.
A week ago today I could feel you inside,
Now there is an emptiness that I cannot abide.

I feel so sad, so empty and unsure,
Should I have done less or maybe some more.
I am a good person and so wanted to be your mother,
Oh God I beg you never take from me another.

The 9th of January, the day that you were due,
Will forever be a day when I will think of you.
How do others conquer this dull and awful pain?
Perhaps there is a reason that from it we will gain.

When will this crying fade away into the past?
How long will this hurt and loneliness last.
Where is the baby that was meant for me to hold?
Who took away the warmth inside and made me feel so cold.

I don't want a stomach that feels so firm and flat,
I want the bump of growth that I can rub and pat.
I used to rub it gently to help my baby sleep,
The baby that was leant to me and never mine to keep.

I know my pain; I can feel it so strongly there,
But there are others with whom this pain I share.
There is your Dad, who cannot grieve the same as me,
But who I know is suffering beyond all possibility.

He has a pain inside that he cannot talk about,
Instead he gets angry and tends to scream and shout.
He isn't as bad or as aggressive as he acts,
Its' just his manly way of not dealing with the facts.

Deep down inside I know he was
looking forward to being your Dad,
And I know with him you would have been so glad.
He is good and kind and loves his children so much,
His gentleness isn't always known but is always in his touch.

From all of us, your brother and sisters whom you never knew,
Your grandparents, aunts and uncles which are more than a few.
We will let you rest in peace and go back to God's care,
But even after this farewell we will always feel you are near.

If God wants you back and wasn't ready to let you go,
Then we will say goodbye as long as you know.
That we wanted you no matter how you were to be,
You didn't have to be 100% to belong to Sean and me.

So God if you are listening, just let us say,
We beg of you please to let the next one stay.
We want you to give us another chance to prove that we are ready,
We are so full of parent love and our relationship is rock steady.

Goodbye from Ger, who should have been your mother
19/06/1998

In Hospital

I sit here in this lonely room
Hoping I will be leaving soon.
The days are long, the nights are worse,
Being sick is such a curse.

I think of all the days gone by,
And spend some time wondering why?
Why I stayed inside on a sunny day?
Watching T.V. instead of going out to play.

Why I thought that school was a bore
And doing homework was such a chore.
Why I thought that parents were mad,
And now when I see them I feel so glad.

Why I thought I didn't have enough to wear
Now if I had to stay in my nightie I just wouldn't care.
I wouldn't care as long as I could be back home,
And didn't have to feel so very much alone.

I promise if I get out soon,
I will be jumping over the moon.
I will do all the housework and study like mad,
Because just to be able to do these things will make me feel glad.

This is probably just hospital mood,
It must have something to do with the food.
It must be designed to keep the energy low
This is something that I just don't know.

I don't know what I'll do when I get out,
I'll probably want to scream and shout.
Scream and shout because I am free,
But then I'll slip back to being the same old me.

So don't worry folks, I'm not gone mad,
Of that I am sure you will be glad.
Hospitals can make you think and think,
So that you can ignore the medicinal stink.

When I'm at home I'll feel sorry for those left behind,
But these memories will soon fade from my mind.
After a few weeks of good homely food,
I will soon be back in a good old mood.

I'll be in the mood to poke some fun,
At my sisters, my dad and my mum.
So you'll all realise what Val's about,
So look out everyone I'M COMING OUT!!

Nancy

Nancy, Oh, Nancy, beloved sister of mine,
I stand and pray at the foot of our shrine.
A shrine that you suggested we build for the town,
From where the mother of God would always look down.

You put me to work and I dug out the lands,
The roadways and rock where the Grotto now stands.
We travelled the country to look at Grottos by the score,
But you made it a joy and never a chore.

We put up the statue and built the surround,
And then we worked hard at clearing the ground.
We planted flowers and trees and built the wall,
And then we let it open to be shared with one and all.

On the 15th August each and every year,
Our friends, family and neighbours would gather for prayer.
You loved to see the young and old out for the day,
With one thing in common and that was to pray.

But now you are gone, we all stand alone,
But the memory of you will always be kept going.
On the 15th August and the 10th of July,
Why you are not here we will always ask why.

We know when we pray you will smile from above,
And shower us all with your kindness and love.
We pray for your soul and hope you are at rest,
Cos' Nancy, Oh, Nancy, you were one of the best.

Sean

At this very moment in my life,
I belong to no-one, I am nobody's wife.
But I have people who belong to me,
Right here and right now the total is three.

I have two little girls and the man I adore,
How could I ever want or need anymore.
Ten years ago my first child Leon came along,
My feelings of love for her will always stay strong.

Then two years ago today you and I met,
I honestly thought, this is as lucky as I get.
Then luck took a leap and now I have another,
Kellie arrived and once more I'm a mother.

I'm the mother of two and the lover of one,
My days on my own have hopefully gone.
I hold all three of you dear to my heart,
To hurt you would truly tear me apart.

Sean I need to thank you so much for all of this,
You have turned my world into a sea full of bliss.
You have given Leon the security that she needs,
You have been like a father without the title deeds.

I know that Kellie is truly a part of you,
But the feeling of sharing a child to me is so new.
Your other two children are also part of my life,
And for them I must thank your darling ex-wife.

I know sometimes I put pressure on your days,
But you have to forgive my moody old ways.
I know that I am changing, I feel more content,
On making your life better, I sure am hell bent.

There is no-one else, there is only you,
You make me believe in a package of two.
I hope that you're as happy as I want you to be,
Because if you're not then I can only blame me.

Mother

Mother, Oh Mother, Oh Mother Divine,
Where is the day when you were all mine.
You left me suddenly, we didn't say goodbye,
And now you will have to allow your big son to cry.

There is so much of my life that I wanted you to share,
And I always believed that you would be there.
My friends have lost their parents and it's made me feel sad,
But why the most precious mother should die
just makes me feel mad.

Since I've found Mairead and love her so much,
With women's lives my feelings are now in touch.
I understand you more now than I've ever done before,
And I was looking forward to getting to know you more.

A dad I soon will be and my love as a parent will then shine through,
My child will probably give me as much pain
and joy as I have given to you.
I could visualise the life of my child as you being their grandmother,
But my child will be deprived as there will never be another.

I wish you were here and I could feel your touch,
This lonely pain is beginning to hurt me too much.
They say time will heal and life moves on,
But they never tell you exactly how you feel when someone so
close is gone.

The family are bearing up but Dad is heartbroken,
His feelings for you were never truly outspoken.
You knew how much he adored you, his one and only life,
The mother of his children, the greatest gift of a wife.

Mairead and I will look after him as best we can,
We'll help him to survive this, as he is my only "Old Man".
I promise I'll look after the others as you would want me to,
And I guarantee I'll never let anyone forget about you.

I have to say goodbye, but we'll talk some other day,
I know you'll always be my mother and never be too far away.
I love you so dearly and leave you to rest,
But always remember that you were the best.

Thank You

The words I needed, were the words you said,
To release this fear inside my head.
I thought that I was going mad,
But you made me realise that I just enjoyed being sad.

I said things to you that I haven't said before,
I hope it's all out, there can't be much more.
There are feelings that I need to share,
And it's great to know that you are always there.

I hold a lot inside my mind,
It felt good to talk with someone so kind.
You made me think and see things right,
And let me see that there is hope in sight.

You are a friend as far as friends go,
You gave up your night to listen to my tales of woe.
For that I cannot thank you enough,
For making me realise that life is not so tough.

I thank you Jo from the bottom of my heart,
For now I know where I must start.
To rebuild a life that's not so dull,
And make my days bright and full.

Thanks.
XXX

SECTION 3
LIFE BEGINS AT FORTY

The Meaning of Life

I remember a time when I thought I had lost my way,
And this is what everyone had to say.
"Live in the now, live for the moment",
How could they not see that I was in torment?

"Torment" can be looked at another way,
"Two are meant" (2RMeant) to face each day.
When you are alone, the day is long,
You feel that your meaning for life is gone.

But if you believe in a higher being,
This will give your life a lot more meaning.
You will take this being with you each day,
And you can never again be alone in any way.

'God' is my being, he is meant for me,
Your being is anything you want it to be.
As long as you believe in my 'God' above,
Your life can only be filled with abundant love.

Love is a feeling of inner joy and peace,
It's what makes you content and full of ease.
You cannot be content if there is hate in your heart,
So by finding love is a good place to start.

You do not have to love another living soul,
You only have to love yourself to make you feel whole.
When you look inside your heart and love who you are,
What you give to the world will be richer by far.

So when you are looking for the 'meaning of life',
Accept that there will always be struggle and strife.
God's life was not easy but he still left beauty behind,
To follow his trail of beauty is how to be found.

So live every day enjoying the beauty all around.
For within it your meaning of life can be found.
It's within your soul and within your heart,
To be a player in this world is your only part.

Enjoy your life and live each day,
Take down your armour, and come on out and play.

Do You??

Where do you find your beauty, is it different to mine?
Do you see it in a rainbow or do you see it all the time?
Do you wake up in the morning, jump out of bed, heart aglow?
Or do you wake up merely wondering how will your day go?

Do you want to see the rainbow, or do you want to see the rain?
Do you want to feel the joy, or do you want to feel the pain?
Do you feel it's not your choice that someone else must know?
That you have no control of how your life truly must go?

Do you hear that voice telling you that you are weak and immature?
When you think you know something, it always knows much more.
Do you decide you want to do something,
but something inside says no?
Does this person inside of you always have a say in where you go?

Do you really know the answer, because the answer lies in you?
And only you can decide exactly what you must do.
The voice inside makes sure you think things through twice,
But what you do with the indecision is totally your choice.

If you listened to the voice and followed what it said,
Then your heart wasn't ready for the first thing in your head.
Take a chance and trust your soul,
With its guidance you will achieve your goal.

You are a strong person, you are as important as you want to be,
Let people know that you are exactly what they see.
I believe you can do anything and even take on something new,
I believe that you are brilliant, but the question is "Do You?"

Valentine's Day

It's February again and love is in the air,
There are hearts and flowers on windows everywhere.
I think of jewellery, clothes and meals,
But you're more into thinking that the car needs new wheels.

I hint and I try to put you in the mood,
I go through the papers and I talk about food.
The food that fills the pages advertising all the menus,
I even go as far as asking which one you'd choose.

You call out your choice and then lick your lips,
Then you say you'd prefer to stay at home with burger and chips.
Burger and chips and kids all around,
Now is the time I decide to stand my ground.

I ask you for money, I'm going into town,
What's the money for you ask with a frown?
I have to get you a present I sweetly declare,
It's nearly Valentine's Day, were you not aware?

I went to the city and bought a deep fat fryer,
I tried to get one locally but the prices were much higher.
I then went to the butchers to buy us some meat,
This is going to be your Valentines treat.

Valentine's Day has arrived at last,
Now I have to organise the rest of my cast.
The kids are washed and dressed and shipped next door,
I light the candles, cook the chips, burgers and do no more.

You come in from work with a grin on your face,
Come on you say you're going to a special place.
You gave me a dress to wear, the best I'd ever seen,
And on treating me like royalty you were dead keen.

Then suddenly it all kicked into place,
As you waited with an anticipated look on your face.
You said where is the present you went out to buy,
Or did you forget about me and not even try.

I showed you the effort I had gone to for you,
Burgers and chips and a table set for two.
It could have been a disaster of a night,
But in the end it turned out alright.

I put on my dress and served up our dinner,
The burger and chips were definitely a winner.
When next year comes around we will try to get it right,
We will do something to please both of us and have a lovely night.

The Prisoner

Morbid, morbid, morbid girl,
Your head is spinning, your hearts in a twirl.
You see everything in a shade too black,
Trust in yourself is something you lack.
You are an outcast, living in an unknown place,
You are a sad misfit in this human race.
Don't be so frightened of being alone,
A constant companion is something unknown.
If people don't like you then don't take it bad,
Study your faults and stop being so sad.
Put on a brave face and take a good look around,
There's a lot of lost happiness that has to be found.
Let people know exactly what they are seeing,
Let them know that you are really a human being.
Don't try to be somebody you definitely are not,
Or the person locked inside you will soon be forgot.
The day that the prisoner wants to break free,
Is a day that people will question who they see.
The way you act is what they will take,
The prisoner will be identified as a definite fake.
You must have some confidence in the very real you,
You must trust yourself in everything that you do.
Don't think too badly of all that you've done,
Living should be a happy treat, not a loaded gun.
If you think that people plan to lock you away,
Tell them you are sorry but you are here to stay.
Stay a little longer and give life a break,
Grab as much fun as you can manage to take.
I am the prisoner and I want to come out,
I want to know what living is really about.
Twenty one years, I've been locked up inside,

I always wondered why I must hide.
Am I so repulsive I must not be seen?
She said I was a misfit, on that I am not keen.
Make way for me now I plan to break free,
I want everyone to know the real me.
If they decide to criticise me bad,
I won't be too sorry. I'll be feeling too glad.
I must not continue this great big bad act,
I must have my freedom; it's something I've lacked.
I am beginning to wonder what is the real me,
Am I the actor or the one who broke free?
The actor who is inside is playing a new game,
She wants me to go back from where I came.
I feel so happy; I could fly in the sky,
If I forget I was a prisoner, I know I'll get by.
The end of my sharing has come and I'm not sad,
In fact my heart is beating glad.
I'm glad to be free of the questions I ask,
I'm glad to be me and take off the mask.

Life Without a Mother??

Life without a mother what would it mean?
The idea of it is something that I am not keen.
You bring us together in a way we wouldn't do,
Because we know that being together is a way of pleasing you.

You are both my friend and my enemy,
You bring out the worst and the best in me.
I need you so much to be in my life,
As much as dad needs you to be his wife.

When I thought about you leaving I felt anger and pain,
The life I know now would never be the same.
You keep me in touch with the family I know,
I know everything they do and everywhere that they go.

If you had decided to give up on us and go your own way,
I would have lost a mother, a friend and a family all in one day.
We would all start to grieve and hurt so much,
We would be so full of pity and fall out of touch.

We have little in common and don't think the same,
But one thing we share is our love and family name.
You have to promise me that you will stay as well as you can,
Because I need my mother and the girls need their Nan.

LifeLine

You might have known me growing up,
or you might have known me growing.
At some point you made an impact on my life,
maybe with you knowing.
You either shared with me my childhood fun and games,
Or you walked with me through my adulthood joys and pains.

There is something in my life that you once did or said,
Something that makes you an important person inside my head.
You influenced my memories, mind and soul in some way,
This influence remains with me each and every day.

We may have played when young, talked or learnt together later on,
But whatever we did is a very special thing that will never be gone.
You are one of the few friends that are special to me,
You are one of my chosen family.

I hope that as I move further along with my destiny,
Your friendship will always remain close to me.
We have now seen the worst and expect the best,
We have learnt at this stage how to deal with the rest.

As you are a special friend in my life,
I would like to be with you in all your struggles and strife.
I'd like to think that at the next stage in our lifeline
That we will grow together and help each other shine.

Just Me

A young girl cried out in pain,
She cried and cried but only in vain.
She wanted to be heard; she wanted to be seen,
To make it obvious she wasn't so keen.

Her mind was in pain, her head was so sore,
The torture within her she could take no more.
She tried to be different; she tried to fit in,
But whatever she tried, she just couldn't win.

She couldn't find her comfort zone,
And she always felt so alone.
She liked to read, she liked to verse,
But these likes of hers had become a curse.

Then she realised that the verse wasn't a sin,
It was her way of expressing what was deep within.
She avoided anger so as to avoid pain,
And then realised that this was in vain.

She should have expressed feelings in a different way,
She should have said what she wanted to say.
She knows from now on she must speak out,
Share her feelings whenever in doubt.

No matter how different she may feel,
To other people out there this life of hers is real.
Everyone is different in their ways of communication
If this book can help you would be my one and only vocation.

To anyone who read this book,
and everyone who cared.

I thank you for taking time,
for now my life you've shared.